lover girl

Check out more of Raegan's work here:

lover girl

raegan fordemwalt

Andrews McMeel
PUBLISHING®

Andrews McMeel Publishing
a division of Andrews McMeel Universal
1130 Walnut Street, Kansas City, Missouri 64106

www.andrewsmcmeel.com

25 26 27 28 29 VEP 10 9 8 7 6 5 4

ISBN: 978-1-5248-9511-2

Library of Congress Control Number: 2024937545

Editor: Danys Mares
Art Director/Designer: Tiffany Meairs
Production Editor: Jasmine Lim
Production Manager: Alex Alfano

ATTENTION: SCHOOLS AND BUSINESSES

Andrews McMeel books are available at quantity discounts with bulk purchase for educational, business, or sales promotional use. For information, please e-mail the Andrews McMeel Publishing Special Sales Department: sales@andrewsmcmeel.com.

for
mikayla, elsa, hayden,
yecenia, alexa, and wilson.

contents

continue to love
more and more

1: beginner's guide to heartbreak

you again

i'm writing about you again.
it's all i really do anymore,
and i don't even mind that you
never think about me.

i used to mind,
but i used to do a lot of things.

lover girl

2:00 am

i love you. it's two in the morning, and
i'm telling you i love you
desperately, pitifully,
as if i had only said it once more,

you'd love me back.
you'd stay.

beginner's guide

i'm struggling to figure out what to do without you.
i hate that: *without you,*
as if there was some *with you* that i wasn't aware
was as temporary as it ended up being.

i've got to move on, i guess,
but crying only helps a little bit, now,
and there's no manual for it.
i've never *moved on* before.

how to fall out of love
(beginner's guide)

lover girl

your stuff

i didn't realize
how little of your stuff i had left.
i thought i had more of you.
i thought i had pulled you inside of my skeleton
and my blood.
i thought each breath you had we shared,
but i just have your dirty laundry instead.

i think you already knew you were gone
before you left.

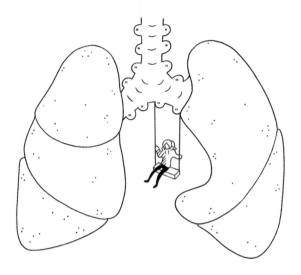

my chest

it's been following me
these past few days.
it's in every step i take,
each bite of food i eat.
in my breath. each time i breathe,
i can feel my chest rattling from
how empty it feels without you.

crying

i hate the way my cheeks feel. puffy.
red. dry. i always used to like crying
during movies or documentaries.
i liked crying.
it made me feel a bit more human.
it's what movies are for, i guess:
tricking us all into feeling happier to be alive.

i used to like crying,
but now i'm relieved to have run out of tears.

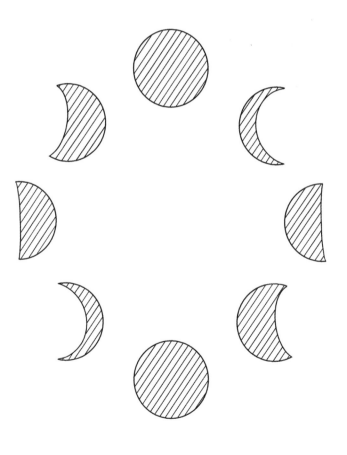

raegan fordemwalt

tomorrow without you

i don't want to wake up anymore.
i don't want tomorrow to come.
no. not another tomorrow without you.

lover girl

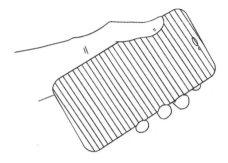

how it ended

i told you *goodnight*
and between the gasps of breath, i told you
i love you
like i had hundreds of times before.
and then you said
i love you too
and i replied
you can't say that anymore.

you paused.
i could hear your bittersweet smile through the phone.
but i still mean it.
i laughed. it felt weird with the tears still on my cheeks
because i knew that you were telling the truth.
i knew that you weren't lying.
i said *goodnight* again
and you were gone.

left for dead

lover girl left when he did.
lover girl left for dead.
she is nothing without him.
lover girl left for dead.

raegan fordemwalt

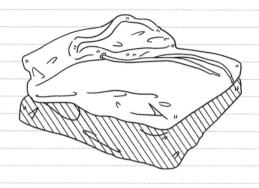

your sweatshirt

i wore your sweatshirt to sleep every night.
i pretended you were holding me.
i covered it in my sweat and tears and
vanilla-scented perfume.
i dreamed you were the prince
and i was the poet and i made
everything become you.

i chewed off the ends of your sweatshirt
like it was mine.
i made it disgusting. i made it like me.
i would have worn it forever
if you would have let me.

i gave it back to you yesterday.

lover girl

you're still here

there are still pieces of you
in my bedroom, in my ceilings, outside.
you're in the sky. you're in the moon.
you're in the places we walked
and in places we never walked.
in all the things i planned to show you
when i didn't know we would end.

♥

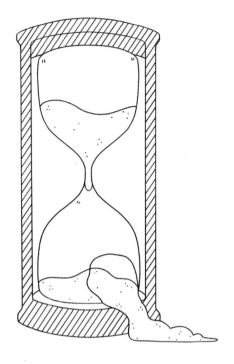

forever

i thought we'd have *forever*
to fix things.

hurt so much

why does it all hurt so much?
why do you hurt so much?

❤

one last kiss

i thought that maybe the taste of my lips
would convince you,
but this is our goodbye, our end.
that's what you said.

it hasn't hit me yet

i don't remember in the mornings.
i keep waking up with a smile.
i'm still dreaming of you.

another chance

maybe if i had told you about the
stars in the sky,
you would have given me another chance.
that's all i needed. i keep thinking:
just another chance.

lover girl

you don't love me anymore

i'm inside out and ripped in two,
and i'm trying to describe it to you,
but you don't love me anymore.

and i know, of course i do,
that i'll sew myself back up
eventually. that's what you told me:
i want you to move on.

but you don't get it.
you don't get how
i'm inside out and ripped in two,
and i'm trying to describe it to you,
but you don't love me anymore.

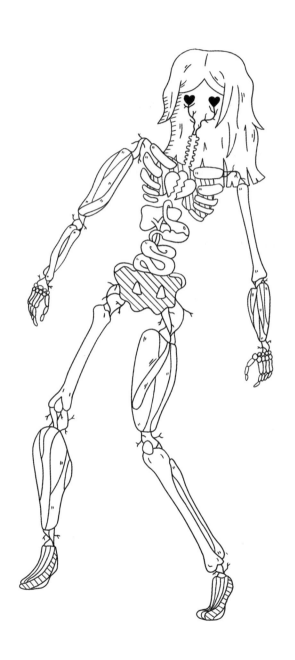

lover girl

what's on your mind

usually, when i thought this,
i'd just call you, ask
what's on your mind?
it always got you talking,
and i liked the sound of your voice.

i can't call you anymore,
but i'm guessing—hoping—
you're thinking about me.

it'd make me feel a little less crazy.

anybody else

i want to text you
so much.

maybe you'd answer.
maybe you'd tell me *i miss you*
and i'd tell you *i miss you too.*

it's funny: i want it so much my mouth salivates
at the thought, but
i don't think it would help either of us.
i think i'd rather it be anyone else.

the new me

i don't like the new me.
i'd trade her back for the memories of the
used to be
that i've made so idealized in my head.

pretending. i am now pretending
that we were right,
that everything was right.
pretending that the girl i was,
the girl i was with you,
was happy.

raegan fordemwalt

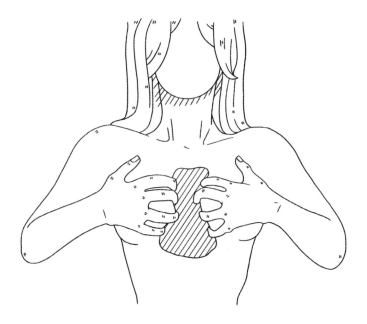

how much i love you

i hate how much i love you.
i hate how i love you so much
it hurts.

i swear it hurts too much to not be real.

25

embarrassed for me

i can't talk to you.
i can't show you my face.
i cried and you could hear me
on the other end of the phone.

i keep wondering what you were thinking.
maybe you were embarrassed for me,
or maybe
you just felt a little sick.

what i did wrong

please just tell me what i did wrong.
i promise i'll fix it.
i'll be better.

anything.

lover girl

sometimes

i have reminders on my phone
to get up
and brush my teeth.
i've been crying almost all the time, but
i've managed to get sleep.
i've started exercising again,
i've started smiling once or twice—
i'm doing so good. i'm doing better,
even still without stars in the sky.

and i can still feel it every day.
i walk around now that you're gone,
but i've been making up my mind
to forgive you.
all i have left is to move on.

because with each reminder that i set,
each poem that i write,
i've been trying. i've been trying to make sure
i'll be alright, and

sometimes i want you to get it.
sometimes i want you to feel as weak,
and i want you to feel the pain i feel.
i want your heart to weep too.

but that's not true.
it's not. for i'm a fool, and
i would let it all go,
i would forget every ache i feel,
if you just returned to my side.

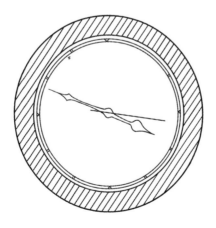

too soon

it's too soon for this.
you're just trying to be nice, but
answering would mean
i've already let you go.

♥

still a comfort

it's getting bad again.
when it's dark, i can taste your kisses on my lips.
i like it: remembering.

it's all i have.

roses

i can't get myself to throw them away yet,
but they're wilting on my countertop,
and their petals crumble when
i put them in my mouth.

maybe that's why you got me roses.
temporary gifts.
they, too, were bound to die.

hold your hand

it's awful.
it's so awful.
i just want to hold your hand
so badly. so *badly,* my love.
i would do anything for it.

i'm so ashamed.

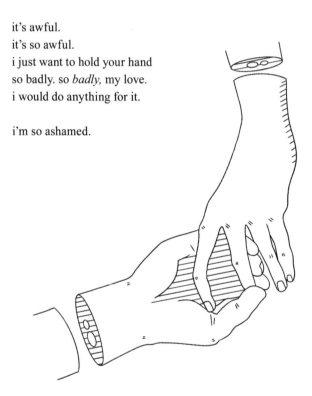

lover girl

sick of the poet girl

i can't help talking about you all the time,
writing my silly poems *all the time.*
i'm sure my friends are sick of it,
sick of me,
but they haven't left yet,
and i'll tire of things to say about you eventually.

i just have to speak it, put it somewhere.
write my poetry, or else
i never loved you at all.

empty

my social media
the photos in my phone
the place in my room
i put the poster you made me for prom.

it's all empty
and i've tried to cover it up
with pictures of my friends
or poetry on sticky notes but
nothing fits like
you did.

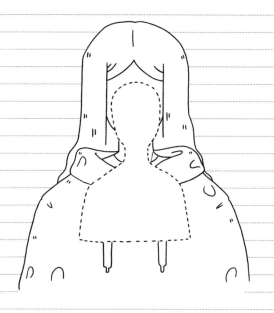

lovesick

i've gotten ill now.
physically ill.
my knees buckle when i'm walking up the stairs.
i'm weak. i can't eat.
i'm starving, but i'm sick.
i get sick when i think of you.
i can't move when i think of you,
but i can't distract my mind from any other thought.
i'm so sick of love and
lovesick for you.

i've lost weight, and
my cheeks burn from the nightmares.
i feel red. i feel dead,
and i know my sickness will pass,
but why did no one ever tell me
that it gets this bad?

thinking of you

i need to write. i have to write.
i have to smile and suck in my stomach,
and i have to stop crying.
god. i have to stop wasting time,
but that's just it.
that's what i always do: i can't stop
wasting my time
still thinking of you.

crush

i feel like i have a crush on you again
because i'm writing poetry i know you'll never read
and scribbling in my diary
to try and get you off my mind,
but it's still
all for you.
always for you.

a deal

i've made a deal with myself:
i'm not going to cry tonight.
i'm not going to let myself look at photos of you
or read back our texts
in the self-destructive way i've learned to lately.
i'm not going to feel any more pain tonight
over you again.

i won't cry.
i promise i won't.

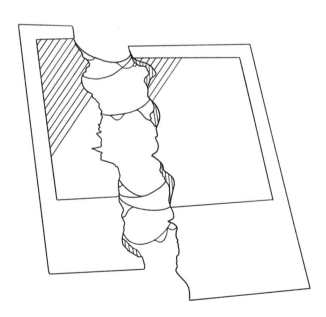

november

why can't it just go back to last november?
everything was *perfect* in november,
and i know you'll tell me every reason it was not,
but i don't believe you.
i won't believe you.

off my mind

i want to get you off my mind,
but, god, i want to see you,
and if you're in my mind, i'm almost there.
you're almost here.
it's almost enough.

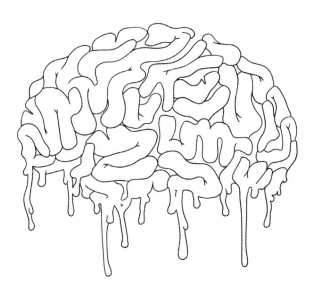

everything

i gave you everything left of me
and i wanted to.

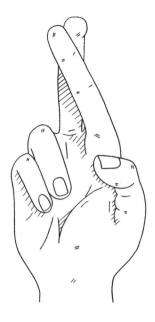

selfish

i'm so selfish because
i wish you lied to me.

i want you to say that you love me.
i don't care if it's not true.
you can pretend.
just say it again.
please just say it again.

pretending that you died

where'd you go?
i feel like i only blinked once
and you were gone.

maybe i should start pretending that you died.
i feel like that thought would hurt less than the thought
that you simply just chose to leave me.

romanticizer

here i am
pitifully romanticizing the breakup

like you care.

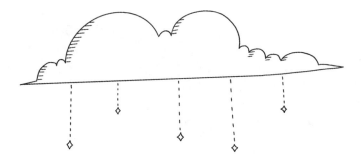

the first poem i wrote about you

it always happens when you smile
or look me in the eyes.
i'd say it's something poetic,
but there are no stars in the sky.

when i get the urge to touch you,
touch your shoulder,
touch your hand,
it feels like i can't help myself,
like i'm waiting to be damned.

i think they call it bittersweet.
the aching stomach, aching chest.
i'd say it hides and moves away,
but i think you know the rest.

oh, i think you know the rest.

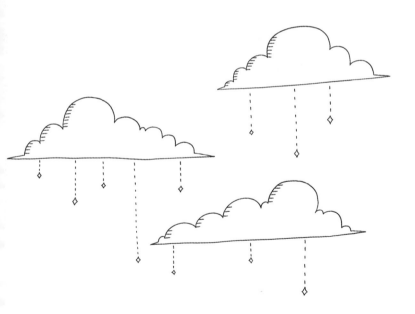

lover girl

i still love you but i don't want to

there's no drug to cure unrequited love,
and if there were, i think i'd take it.
the strongest painkiller ever made.
not to cure a cold or a broken bone,
but to cure a broken heart.

but life couldn't be that simple, could it?
there's no magic remedy out there.
there's just me and my poems and my thoughts.
i'm watching the clock.
they say time heals heartbreak, but
it hasn't kicked in yet.
i wish i knew when time would
start working on me.

♥

why do i still want you?

you left me
and i watched.
that should be the end of it, shouldn't it?
but no, of course not.
a *lover girl.*
i almost forgot.

of course i can't let it go yet.

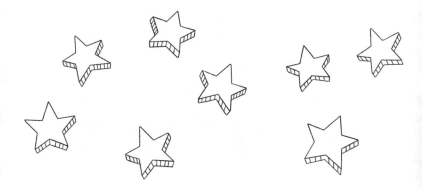

i loved you more than poetry

i've always been more of a fool
than a girl. or maybe those just go together
when you're me.
either way, i became a fool for poetry
march 4th, 2020.
i started writing. the world was my muse. i was so
obsessed, looking back.
i covered my entire wall in
sticky notes, things that i wrote.
i didn't have very many friends back then,
but i don't remember minding.
i had my poetry, the words i wrote every day,
but i never thought of myself as a poet.
no, i was just me.

raegan fordemwalt

i wrote two poems a day. i still do,
and for the past two years, since we met,
nearly all of those poems have been about you.

you told me once, long ago,
that you loved me more than music,
and i told you in return that
i loved you more than the stars in the sky.

it's crazy, right? but
you were all that was on my mind.
i hated you. i adored you. i envied you,
and i wrote down every word.
i became a fool for you
march 4th, 2021,
and i loved you as i came undone.

and i hate myself because
i would have given all my poems up for you.
i think i've written nearly three thousand by now.
i would have scraped the words clean off my soul.
i would have burnt my books
to burn away your cold.

♥

lover girl

i told you once, long ago,
that i loved you more than the *stars in the sky,*
but it was a lie
because i loved you more than
my poetry, my dreams.
i loved you more than i loved me.

i loved you enough to
want to hand you the world if i could,
but the craziest part is that i still would.

my words are the only things that have
been by my side all this time.
they're where i go late at night.
they make me something.
they make me *me,*
but if i could trade them all for
your love again,
i'd be too weak to say no.

and of course it would never work out like that.
i'd want you, but we'd still be our worst
because we didn't fit. we didn't work out,
and you were just the one who noticed it first.

i loved you more than poetry.
i loved you more,
and that's how everyone like us ends, after all.

i loved you more.

2: lover girl

lover girl

lover girl can't fall asleep without a phone call
and can't eat until he tells her it's okay.

she needs him. needs to drink him.
needs to kiss him, keep him, be him,
for poor lover girl
can't fall asleep without a phone call
and can't eat until he tells her it's okay.

look at her. what a pity.
she's so in love.

she calls it love.

never again

i am probably
never going to talk to you again.
you're dead in my body, dead in my heart.
you're dead.
and we're too different than we were then
because the man i loved is dead.

i am never going to see you again,
and i have to be okay with that.
how can i be okay with that?

old poems

i'm too scared to look at my old poems.
they're all about love.
it's always all about love.

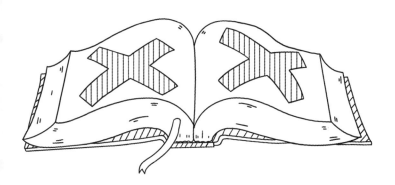

morning depression

when i can't find a reason to wake up,
i get up anyways.
there's bound to be a reason out there somewhere,
isn't there?

i think i've stopped wanting you.
now i'm just tired.

i'm so scared i'll never be in love again.
i get most scared in the mornings
because i used to wake up and
wish for your voice, but
now i just wake up and wish for nothing.

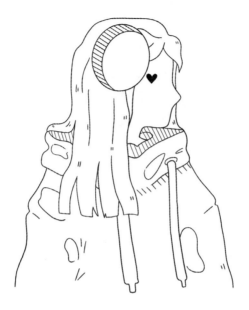

days that come

there are days that come
rarely
when not a single thought of you
crosses my mind.

lover girl

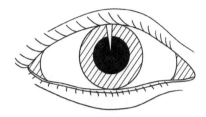

98%

the truth is
i knew we weren't going to work out.
i mean, it's high school,
but there was always a part of my mind that thought
we'd be the *exception.*
2% of high school sweethearts get married.
why couldn't that be us too?
it's not a rule,
and i'm a good kid. i'm a good girl
who does well in school and follows the rules.
i deserved a high school sweetheart.
i wanted a love story. i wanted to be the couple
others were jealous of.

but now look at us.
a statistic. a number. 98%.
we're the trendsetters,
just one of thousands of other couples who
broke up this summer. just like them.
it cheapens it.
like my love for you didn't feel like i could
travel around the world. like the love i had
was somehow born to be flawed.

but it's just high school, right?

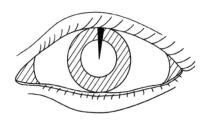

first weekend alone

i made it through my first weekend alone
since you left me.
since then, i've kept busy.
school. work. doing everything and nothing,
but i've had to learn to like the party of just me.
a weekend of just me.

pity party. hooray.
it's too hot outside for ice-cream cake.
the summer's drowning me,
and i'll stay inside
with my little bed, my little heart,
trying to bring it back to life.

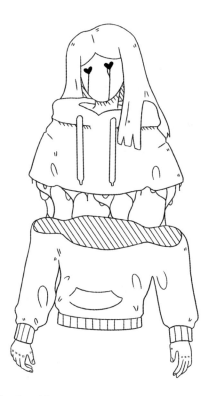

hands shoulders eyes

i'm always here, split in two again,
crying alone with just the company of
my hands, shoulders, and eyes.
i hate them, but maybe by tomorrow,
if i keep crying,
it'll mean i'll be okay again.

lover girl

fever dreams

i am tender, squishy, weak.
i am malleable, pliable. i am putty, and
i am melting into the couch,
but i just wish i was
melting into you.

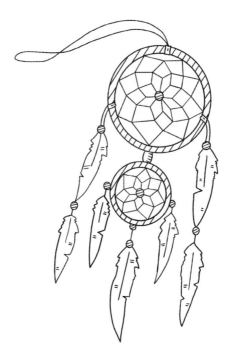

dream catcher

the dream catcher still hasn't been able to
keep you away.

during the days, i can avoid you,
but once the sky falls and
there's no longer the light to remind me
that you're gone,
you return. you smile and i love you still.

with you

even knowing how unhappy we became,
i'd still, my love, rather be miserable with you
than miserable without you.

weather

it's pouring outside and
i always look prettier when it rains or
when i'm crying.
i think it's because of my eyes.
i keep feeling like the rain has no right
being so beautiful when i'm sad,
but the rain doesn't care.
why should it?
it's just the rain.

lover girl

our love story

you were the subject
of every poem i wrote.
god, i made a love story out of
scribbled *i love you*s and
the princess bride quotes.

i wanted you to stay so badly.
i wanted the end of the world, and
i wanted you like i needed to,

but just writing down how you love me
doesn't make it true.

i wanted a happy ending,
and i wanted it to be you.

other boys

i still feel some sort of loyalty to you.
i can't look at other boys.
i don't want to. i have you.

and i'm telling myself
i'm just *not ready* yet,
that i need more time.

but i think i'm just waiting
for you to change your mind.

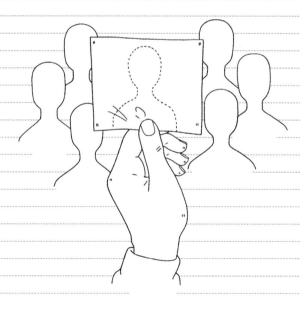

i don't believe in shooting stars

i don't believe in shooting stars,
fallen eyelashes,
making wishes under tunnels,
or blowing out birthday candles.
i don't believe in them, but i can't help
wishing on them anyways.
it's addicting: wishing, wanting.
i feel like i deserve better. i love myself enough
to know i deserve better,
but it never works, does it?

for every superstition i follow for good luck,
my good luck never comes.

i don't believe in shooting stars, but
i want to. my god, i want to.

raegan fordemwalt

sound

it's quiet here.
sometimes, in the places where i've
removed all the noise,
time stops. you are gone like you were never
even mine.

i miss you most in the quiet places.
i miss you most when i miss sound.

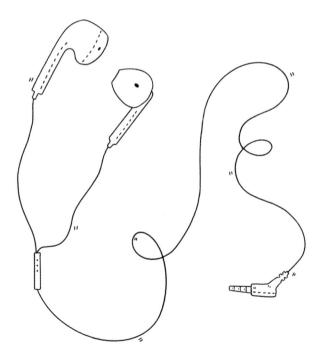

lover girl

when i hear your name

my heart drops every time i hear your name now
because it's never good news,
at least nothing that i'd ever want to hear.

insecure

i've stopped asking my friends
what's on your mind?
i've stopped texting past nine
and i've stopped loving them too much
like i did to you.

i'm so paranoid now.
i'm so paranoid
they'll leave me too.

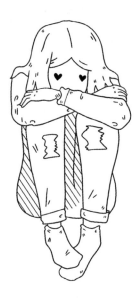

lover girl

never

i don't mean to watch you,
but i always tend to notice everything you do.
it hurts too much.
i don't even know why.
i think it's just the thought that i'll never
love another boy the way i loved you
and that you don't feel the same.

seeing you again

i saw you in person again, and
i didn't feel my heart break.
i wasn't surprised. i wasn't even nervous!
i saw you. i talked to you, and it felt normal.
i felt okay.

i'm used to being around you, i guess,
or maybe i just
used to be.

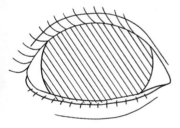
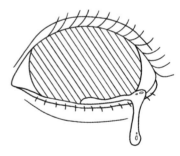

the most

my therapist told me yesterday that
the next person i'm with, i will love more.
and should there be another boy after him,
i will love him more.
and should there be another, i will love him more
and then more and somehow more
until i finally find the person
i will love the most. the most out of them all.

and isn't that just romantic?
because i can't imagine anyone else.
i don't want anyone else.
i love you the most.
you are my most,
and how could i ever want someone who
i'd love more than you?

how could she ever tell me that i'll love someone
more than you
when she doesn't get it?
she doesn't understand that there will be no *most*.
there's no most without you.

what you didn't like about me

i can't help focusing on the things you
didn't like about me.
i don't want to change,
but if i did,
would it make it all go away?

would you have stayed?

chasing

i'm sick of chasing after people.
if they wanted to,
they'd call me.

that's all it is, isn't it?

the end to a bad thing

of course i remember
how we fought all the time,
and this breakup,
any breakup,
is really just the end to a bad thing.
i know that.
i know we're better off without each other,
but it doesn't make me miss you any less.
it doesn't make me any less pitiful
without you.

codependent love

i don't think codependent is the right word.
codependent implies you depended on me.
but i feel toxic—
i wish you did.
i wish, like me, you couldn't handle
the thought of being apart.
i wanted a codependent love.

lover girl

normally

normally, on a day like this,
i would have been with you,
or i would have been calling you, and
we'd be playing some online game.

normally, we'd get bored of it and just start talking,
and i'd tell you about my day, and you'd listen
before you'd say you love me,
and we'd fall asleep.

❤

but i didn't even notice when normal changed.
when the normal became
the arguing.
normal became a text instead of a call
until there was no more text to send.
normal became the crying and the
accusations. it became clinging to an
i love you too.

and now normal is just me,
but i have no more tears left to cry.

and isn't that funny?
that my normal used to just be
you and i.

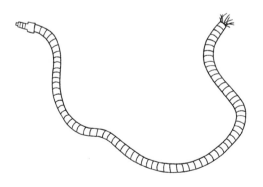

lover girl

poems you'll never see

i never showed you many of my poems
even when i had the chance to.
i don't know why it's the only thing
i want to do now.

raegan fordemwalt

driving

i have to play music to fill the silence,
but i can't play some songs anymore.
i can't play my favorites
because they were your favorites too.

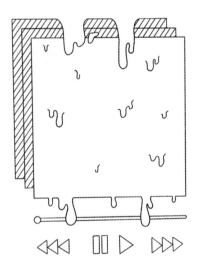

puppy love

i didn't love like a dog.
i swear it hurt more than that. i'm not just a kid,
i was in *love.* love just as real as theirs.
i swear it's painful enough to be true.

but when i grow older,
i know my story will be the same.
i'll hear the same words my mother told me
of her first love. she said,
we just didn't know any better,
of course not,
we were only seventeen.

satellite

i could travel to space,
i could go to the moon,
but i'd still find you in the satellite,
the solar system,
and i'd still find you in the stars.

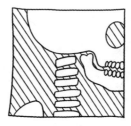

i love too hard

i love too hard.
i do.
i send you every little detail about my life
hourly
from a picture of my cat to
the dirt on my brand-new shoes.
i overwhelm you.
i hold your hand whenever you're near.
i take photos of us
like if i don't you'd disappear.
i stay over every other night
and i tell you i'm anxious
but i just like waking up by your side.

you're every thought that's on my mind,
and i love it, you know,
because i love you, and why wouldn't i
want to keep thinking about you?

i'm sorry. i'm sorry.
i'm sorry, my love.
i'm sorry.

lover girl

"she'll be fine"

i wonder what my friends think. i wonder
if they think it's just a spell.
oh, she'll be fine.
she always is, haven't you noticed?
she's not the type to cry all the time.

oh, she'll be fine, they think.
she'll end up fine.
she's got her poetry,
she'll be alright.

the worst part is   .
i hope they're right.

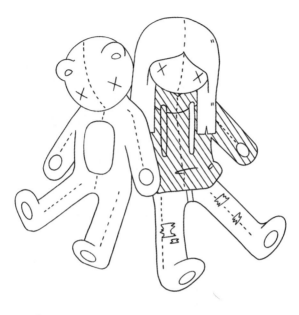

just for one

i've nobody to invite.
only lonely old me.
lonely little me.

i wanted you.
i just wanted you
and now that you're gone
i've got the world at my fingertips but
nothing in my palm.

lonely little me
throws a party just for one.

lover girl

visceral

i see you and my heart burns.
it crawls out of me and
slips between my breasts.
it dies by the weight of my body
and broken bones.

my hands start shaking and my throat constricts
and for a moment i forget—

i'm back there in the passenger seat of your car
i'm holding up your phone for directions
still mixing up my lefts and rights.
you make a turn. i look down and
the polaroid picture of us from new year's
falls from your center console.

♥

i can't believe you still have this

i only kept it because you looked ridiculous—

i love you. i love you like
i need you.

my heart burns and i only saw you for a second.

lover girl can't eat.

to be loved again

i just want to be loved again.
i just want what i used to have.

and it's a lie because
i don't care if you love me.
i don't care if you do because
if we just spoke,
that'd be enough.
maybe it'd be enough.

a thousand poems

i am surrounded by every pretty thing
i wrote for you.
i am drowning in my own words like
the fool i knew i was.

she's so in love. lover girl calls it love.

i wanted to write you a thousand poems,

and i did.

lover girl

already know

why can't i just be happy again
and have all the people i love
love me back?
why couldn't we have just worked out
and kept working out?
why did you leave?
why did you go?

but i guess i shouldn't ask.
i already know.
of course i already know.

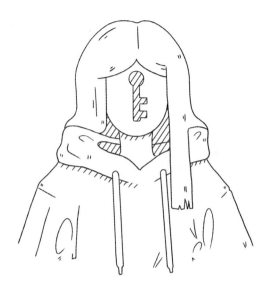

things you can't do

i wonder if you, too, have music you can't
listen to anymore,
places you can't go,
people you can't talk to,
clothes you can't wear.

i wonder if you notice that i'm gone.
i hope you notice i'm not there.

desperate

i wanted to eat you
and spit you out and
kiss you and be you.

i wanted to write you the world.

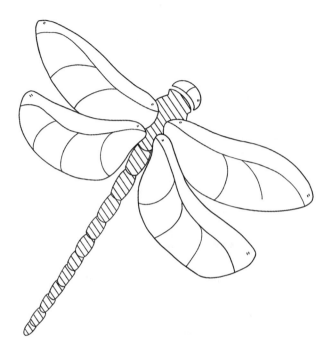

summer dragonflies

i picture your face
and see a stranger, but
the summer shows me dragonflies.
just dragonflies.

i still catch them between my fingers
like i did when you were mine.

lover girl

my heart is tired

my heart is tired.
it beat loud and then it stopped.
you were here then you were not.

whiplash. another car crash.
my life didn't feel as crazy
when you were always keeping me steady.

my heart is tired of beating for you
and beating for people who
don't love me anymore.

my heart is too tired to keep hurting.

poem about the rain

you told me once, a year ago,
to write a poem about the rain.
do you remember that? i hope you do.

well, here it is, my darling,
but i hope you remember how it ended too.

lover girl

your poems

you hated writing poetry.
despised it. you were never good with
words or rhymes, and it
took up too much of your time.
but you still wrote for me.
i still have your
sweet love poems you toiled over
just because you knew i liked them.

you used to tell me you would do
anything for me,

and it used to be true.

❤

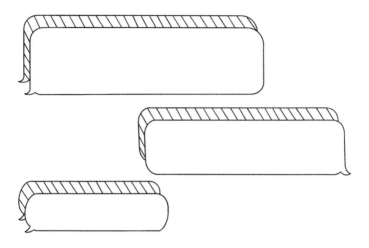

really real love

i finally deleted your name from my contacts list.

i was putting it off for a long time.
i kept thinking that if i didn't delete it,
it was proof that we were really something.

it would be proof if someone asked me
if you really loved me.
of course you did. you told me in all capital letters.
you told me with heart emojis.
every single one, a hundred times.

lover girl

you told me it spelled wrong because you were typing
it too fast
and sending me your love
as much as you possibly could.
you told me you loved me every night without fail,
every time we called.
you sent me pictures of cats and
wrote my name twenty times
until i picked up my phone.
it was juvenile, innocent.
it was everything i wanted,
and everything i miss.

there's so much proof, right here,
in all these messages. you really loved me.
you loved me just as much as i loved you.
really real love. *how cute.*

but here i am now, deleting your picture
from my phone,
deleting the hearts after your name.
here i am now, deleting your name
like you were nothing but a wrong number.

i still can't believe it, even seeing it written out
under my own screen name hundreds of times.
seeing me tell you *i love you* hundreds of times.

i can't believe it.

how, possibly, could i love someone so much
and let them leave me?
how, possibly, could you love me so much,
and then just

not at all?

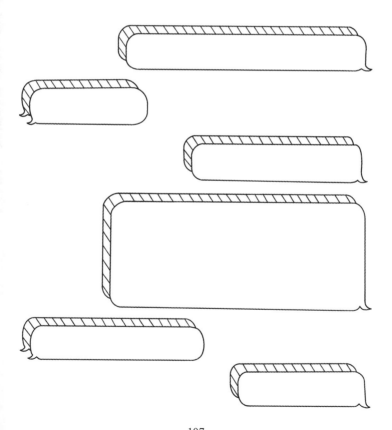

upon the stars

i wished upon the stars today.
it felt silly to do so, but
they were too pretty not to.
and i don't think i phrased it right, my wishing.
i don't think the stars will listen.

but i wished for love
like the love you and i had.
i wished for that.
not with you, of course not,
but i just wanted to be wanted again like
you wanted me and i wanted you.

and the stars didn't hear me,
but at least i got it off my mind.

the mirror

maybe, on the other side of the mirror,
you're thinking of me too,
but i hope not. i don't think you should.

it does neither of us any good.

lover girl isn't good at being alone

i'm not happy anymore,
and it feels like i won't be happy again
until i fall in love.

i've grown addicted to love
(lover girl isn't good at being alone),
and i know, logically, i do not need the kiss of
another pair of lips
to make me feel as if i'm alive,
but the last time i felt alive
was when i was with you.
i hate it:
it's been nothing ever since you left.

codependent baby me.
lover girl isn't good at being alone.

comfort

sometimes, i don't want to get over it.
heartbreak is a comfort,
and it ending would mean
you're really gone.

me and you

there's me. there's you.
there's the end of the world,
but it's just you and i,
isn't it?
it's always just been us
at the end.

bittersweet, again

and i ask
why does falling out of love
feel the same as falling into it?
why am i seeing the *stars in the sky,*
and why does it feel like a lie i'll soon forget?

3: someone else

what do they have

what do they have that i don't?
what did i do wrong?

what do they have?
what do they have?
what do they have?

mine to lose

i can't sleep anymore.
i can't eat.
it's like it's happening all over again.
it's like you're leaving me all over again.

except this time
you weren't even mine to lose.

you're just falling in love again

i don't like it,
but it's not like you owe me anything.
you're just falling in love again.
it shouldn't be as big a deal as it feels.

that's all it is, all it should be,
but i'm a fool and
i can't stop repeating it because

you're just falling in love again.

lover girl

i love you more

i really did love you more.
i hate that.

everyone

before this all,
i could fool myself into thinking
it wasn't just *me* you didn't want,
it was everyone.

but that wasn't true.
silly little lover girl,
of course it wasn't true.

lover girl

who i'm supposed to be

my face is clay in my dreams,
and i can pinch it, pull it outward, and
shape my cheeks.
i feel like you'd like me more
if only i shaped my cheeks
just like hers.

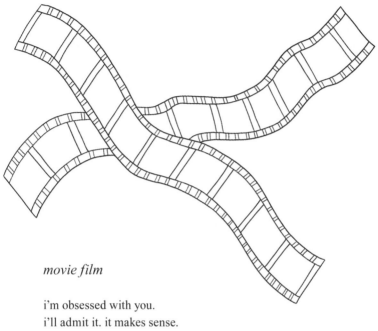

movie film

i'm obsessed with you.
i'll admit it. it makes sense.
i was just as obsessed with you before you left.

but now i want a movie of your life.
a film.
a camera following you everywhere you go and
answering all the questions i have of
what you're doing and where you are.
are you with them?

are you with them?
god. are you?
i want to know.

perfect for you

maybe it would hurt less
if she wasn't perfect for you
in the way i could never be.

pitiful

it would be embarrassing to tell you
how horrifically i sobbed into
my brother's arms
just because i saw her wearing your shirt.

lover girl

if she didn't exist

maybe by now
if she didn't exist
you'd have taken me back.
you'd have realized your *mistake*
you'd apologize and
god, you'd take me back.

but she ruined it.
she loved you and ruined it all.

i can keep telling myself it's her fault
and eventually, one day soon
it might even make me feel better.

need to know

i want to see every text message you sent her,
listen in on every time you called her,
know every time you kissed her.
i want to see out of her eyes and into yours
just one more time.

i want to know—need to know *how.*
how did it happen?
how did you fall in love with someone else?

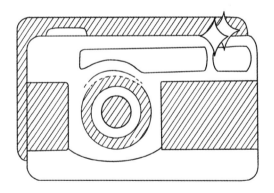

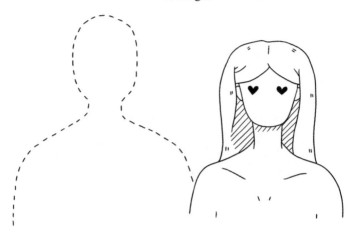

someone else

your someone else
is pretty.
she's everything i think you'd like,
and i know you, and i
know how you're pining.

it's awful because
of course i can imagine you and her.
i can see you kissing her temple
in the way you used to do
to me.
you're calling her at night
and picking her up for concerts and picnics
and every place i know you like.

i can imagine you in love with her
so easily. your love with her
is so much more natural than yours with me.

i guess it hurts because i can't imagine
my life in love with any other boy.
i can't see myself with a someone
other than you.

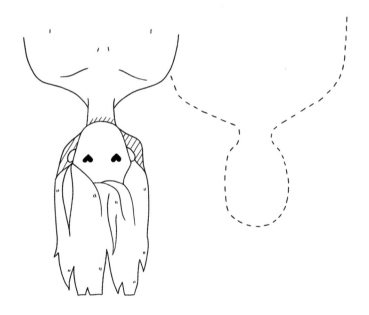

lover girl

evil

and some evil part of me
wishes you the worst.
i hope your new love is not as good.
i hope you still want me
and when you're with her
you look for how i made you feel
in every touch.

it's all i want for you to miss me,
but that's not how love works.

butterflies

i can't stand the thought of you,
the sight of you.
the butterflies in my stomach have turned to blades.
they slice me up.

go away.
make these feelings go away.

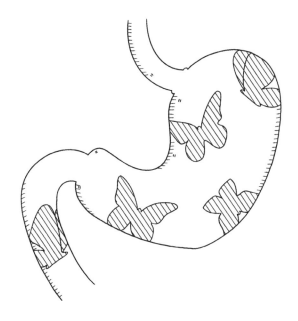

on purpose

it feels like it's on purpose.
what a stupid thing to think.
i feel like a narcissist.
i feel like a liar and a cheat,
even though
love never happens on purpose.

i watch you and her,
and i watch me.

intruding

i don't know you anymore,
even though i used to know you
better than anyone else in the world.

maybe she knows you the best now.
i feel like an intruder,
still loving you.
stranger me.

wishing. wishing. wishing.

maybe now you're playing our song for her.
maybe now you're driving her around downtown
like you always promised you would do with me.
you're letting her wear your clothes, and
i don't ever cross your mind,
like i was never even there.

maybe now you feel the same
as you did with me,
while i'm here, still pitifully thinking about you.
wishing. wishing. wishing.

lover girl calls it love.

every day

i want to be her, but
only because she can text you and you'd reply.

she gets to talk to you *every day.*
(i've forgotten what it's like.)

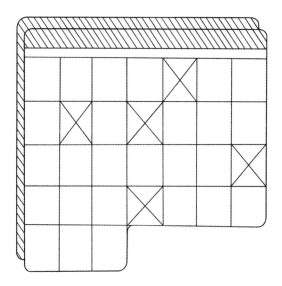

lover girl

the man you'd never be for me

why are you
everything i wanted you to be
now that you're gone?
why does she get
the man you'd never be for me?

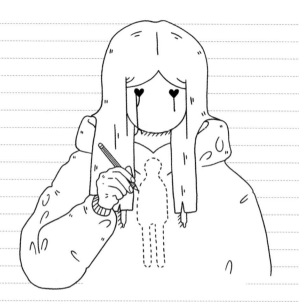

terrible things

i want to write terrible things about you.
i want to write about how you
mistreated me or cheated on me,
abused me or used me.
i want to write about you and
not feel guilty, but

you just loved me once
and then didn't.

lover girl

her face

i'm afraid to look at her face now.
i keep noticing her, noticing when she's there.
my stare makes heat on her back, but
i'm afraid to look at her mouth and nose and
eyes because
she's so pretty,
and it makes me want to cry.

the same

i can't really blame her for falling for you.
i fell for you too.

i get it. she and i are more alike than
anybody else, i guess.
we are the same.

touching

i can't stop thinking about
her touching you and you touching her.
her hands. her hips.
her hair.

her hands.
her hands.
her hands.

heartbeat

my heart stopped beating
when yours started,
as if it knew, somehow, already,
that this would be the death of me.

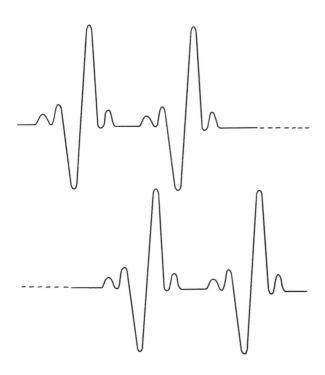

lover girl

full names

your full names repeat inside my head like
i'm about to forget them.

i torture myself in my loving of you,
but i'm a poet and a fool.
it's what we do.

cut my hair

i'm not like her.
well, i guess i am. it's more like
all the things that make you like her
i will never be.

and my mom says i shouldn't compare
myself to her, but i can't help it.

i can't help it.
maybe i should cut my hair.

just seconds

i wanted to spend every second
you would let me
with you.

i keep going back to each one, each instance,
each second when i touched your lips
or felt your hand on my hips.
they're becoming a rarity now in my memories
the more you fade away.

i stole every second of yours
that you let me. i pried them from your schedule
and from your life.
i'm so selfish.
i want all the seconds you give to her
to be given to me instead.

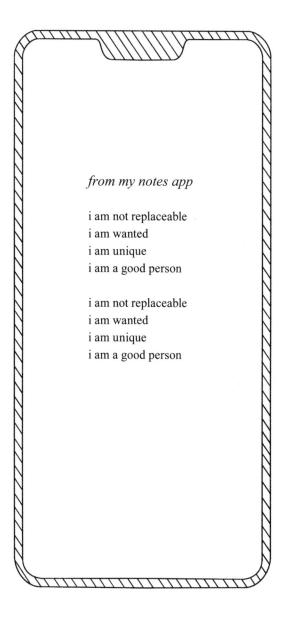

from my notes app

i am not replaceable
i am wanted
i am unique
i am a good person

i am not replaceable
i am wanted
i am unique
i am a good person

lover girl

why do you

i just want to be loved and love again.
i liked it. i miss it,
but you didn't like it enough to stay,
so why, now, do you have it
and i don't?

but i guess it's love.
it's just love.

raegan fordemwalt

unlovable

what if i'm just
unlovable?

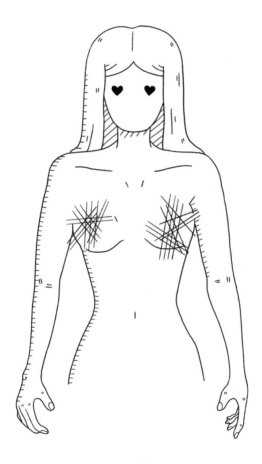

♥

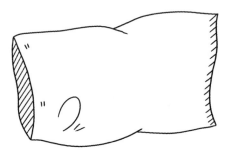

what bothers me

it's not the fact that you're kissing her that
bothers me.
i mean, it does bother me, but it's more like
i bet you're staring up at your ceiling at night,
smiling, giggling,
thinking about her
at the same time that i'm staring up at my ceiling,
tears streaming onto my pillow,
thinking about you.

she gives you butterflies.
you're leaning onto her shoulder and
shaking your head at her jokes,
and you're staring up at your ceiling late at night.

that's what bothers me the most.

lucky

you're so lucky to not be stuck with
someone like me.

black cars

every time i see a black car
i imagine it's hers, and
i imagine she's driving to your house.
her parents told her she had to be home by nine.

but it's love.
you're kissing her and saying
five more minutes. stay.

she never makes it home by nine,
and i never cross your mind.

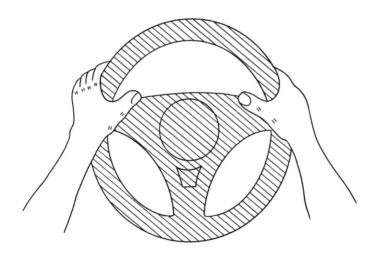

lover girl

what if she loves you?

i giggled over your arms and
the way you talked to your dogs.
i fawned over pictures of us
and got butterflies every time you kissed me
like you were still just my crush.

i wonder if she has a crush on you now—
is she kicking her feet reading a text from you?
is she talking about you to her friends?
does she love you just as much
as i once did?

what if she's a lover girl too?

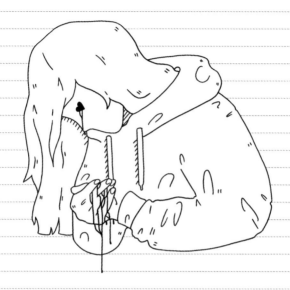

victim

i can't keep pretending i'm some
victim of your love just because
i loved you once and did it wrong
and you found someone who
loved you right.
i'm no victim of that.
you broke up with me. you can do
whatever you like,
but i'm a writer and i romanticize.

you put this knife inside of my heart, but
instead of taking it out,

i twisted it.

lover girl

wearing the same clothes

i've started wearing the same clothes as her,
and i know you don't notice,
but i keep thinking, if i change myself
to be the same,
you'll like me just as much.

or maybe it's worse.
maybe some messed-up part of me just wants to
wear it better,
outdo her,
even though i know i never will.
it will never be enough.

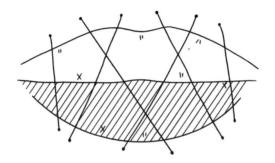

i've not kissed you in months

your new love has
absolutely nothing to do with me.
i don't matter in your story anymore,
your love story,
because i've not kissed you in months.
that's her now.

and she'll kiss you every day for
months and months more.

lover girl

idea of her in my head

i have this idea of her in my head.
what my friends have told me,
what i've seen on her social media,
who i think she is
and who i know you are.

i am pathetic because
this idea i've made of her,
i talk to. i speak with her in my mind.
i ask her what you're doing and
how you are.
i make her ugly and mean
and unkind,
everything she's not,
like fabricating her flaws would cause
my own to go away.

the queen

you and her are everywhere,
but i'm learning to not be afraid of the bees
and their honey
and their sting.

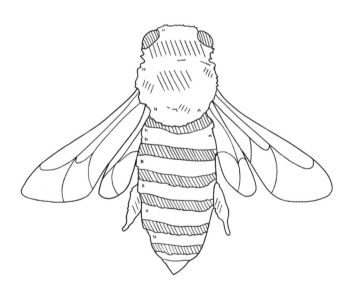

lover girl

here

i shouldn't be here.
your life would be so much easier should
i leave the planet, leave the school.

i'm a black hole.
not meant to touch, not meant for love.
but if only i weren't here, you might
forgive me.

all about me

why does it feel like it's all about me?
of course it's not.
i know that. i know that,
but i can feel you all around me,
inside of me,
her and you, touching me,
even though you never meant it.
you never meant it to hurt.

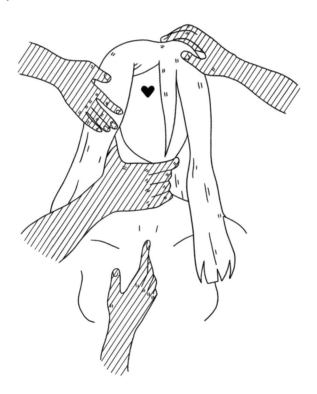

happy

why can't you just be happy, and
why can't i just be happy for you?

it's just that simple, isn't it?
it always has been.

easier

it's getting
easier and easier
to stop thinking about you
when i know you're thinking of someone else.

lover girl

when you say you love her

i hope i'm still with you
when you're around her.
i hope when you kiss her, you think of me.
she and i have a lot in common, and
i hope you like her because she's like me.

and when you say you love her,
i hope i am still there, even if only a little bit,
in your mind.

and of course i don't mean you don't mean it
when you say you love her.
i know you do. you wouldn't say it
if you didn't know it for sure.

but i hope when you say you love her,
i am under every word.
when you say you love her,
please don't forget you loved me first.

i can hope, but i know i'll let it go,
and i know you already have.

a little bit

i only thought of you and me
a little bit today.

i feel like i can breathe.

what you wanted

i still want the best for you.
it's true.

i hope you got the life you wanted,
the one you were looking for.
i hope she's everything. i hope she's pretty.
i hope she's kind.
i really hope she is.

even if i wasn't it,
i really hope she is.

i still want the best for you.
i really do.

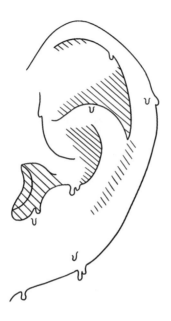

the less i know

the less i know about you,
the less i know about you two,
the better i feel.

watching you fall in love

it reminds me of the beginning.
i liked you *so much.*

i don't remember how i fell in love with you.
i don't think that's something easy to place,
but it seems so easy, watching you and her now.
i knew it. i could see your love for her
in the way you held her hand just as tight
as you used to hold mine.

i'm thinking of your beginning.
i know she bought you flowers.
i wonder if you took her to the park we went to
and if you kissed her under a clouded sky for
your first time.
i wonder if you like her *so much* now.

i feel a bittersweet smile touch my lips.

why is love always so beautiful? i ask,
but i already know, and you're already gone.

happy

in some weird way
seeing you happy still makes me happy
because she and i have a lot in common:
we both want the best for you.
and i used to think that the *best* was me,
but seeing you happy
has proved me so wrong.

stars in her eyes

i traded the stars for you,
but it seems pointless, keeping them away,
when you have your own stars in the sky,
and she has stars in her eyes
all the same.

i'm almost there. i'm almost there.
can you feel it?
i'm almost there.

♥

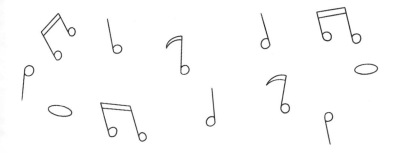

i don't think i love you anymore

i don't think i love you anymore.
i spent so long trying not to,
and i thought it would be a relief,
not loving you,
but here i am and i just feel nothing at all.

when it happened, it was quiet.
i was alone in my room, listening to
last words of a shooting star by mitski
and applying mascara slowly and carefully like
i wasn't going to take it off only twenty minutes later
before i went to bed.
and i realized, staring at myself in my dirty mirror, that
i hadn't thought about you all afternoon.

lover girl

and that this new, sudden thought i had of not thinking
about you
did not bring me any new distress.
it did not hurt me any more to think about it.
and as mitski sang of liberty bells
and working days,
i whispered to my empty room,
i don't love you anymore,
and it felt true.

and now, i'm here
writing this poem and wondering
why i'm not happy about it
why it just makes me feel cold and empty.
i've worked for so long trying to not love you,
so why am i not smiling now that i don't?
why can't i get a grin to show?

my mind goes back to the last time
i had laughed, really laughed, and
i was with my friends watching
the original *scream,*
even though it came out twenty-six years ago.

i think back to that, and i smile again.

i realize:
maybe not loving you won't make me happy.
it's loving the rest of the world,
it's loving me,
that will.

4: the stars in the sky

the top of the world

we made it to the top of the world.
here, on this stupid hill
in this stupid park, and
it's only 8:30 at night, and
the sun's already set, but
i can see the stars.

they're back.

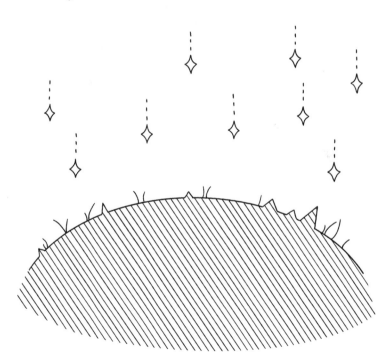

each place we kissed

i won't ever forget the first time we kissed
or each place where we did,
but i won't have to, will i?
they can stay memories,
even if you and i stay apart.

proof

heartbreak is simply proof
that my love,
my heart,
was strong enough to hurt me back.

i wear my broken heart on my sleeve.
i am proud to have loved.

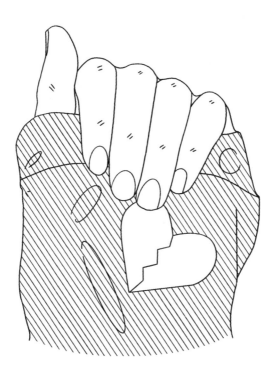

a thank you

you let me go because you knew
i would never have done the same for you.

raegan fordemwalt

day by day

it hurts a little less every day.
slowly, it'll stop hurting.
slowly, it'll go away.

and i can take as long as i wish
to let you go.

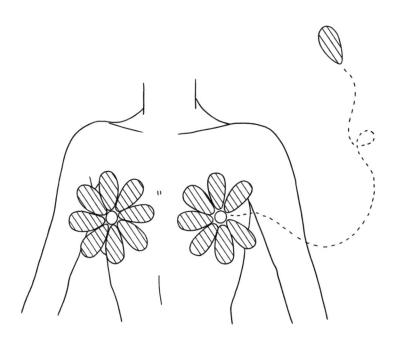

grief

grief only hurts because i loved.

i grieved over us so much,
i ripped myself inside out and
sewed my body back
together again.

but there's still something
so good about that, i think:
how much i loved.

♥

the heart

isn't it fascinating how
the heart,
even after being broken and bruised,
being torn in two,
is still able to beat for a body to use,
to make it run and move?

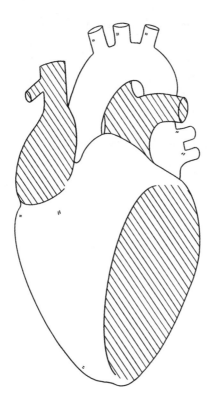

writing helps

i am writing all the words i could never say to you,
confessions onto just a screen in my hand.
writing how much i hate you and love you
and hate that i loved you—
writing helps me finally let it out of my head.

it's embarrassing: my darkest thoughts
i'll tell nobody else that i've found.
secrets i hold that only feel real after
i've written them down.

when i can't say the things that
i'll tell nobody else,
writing helps.

♥

someday

someday,
one day,
you'll be the furthest thing from my mind,
and i won't feel anything but contentment
at the thought of you.

girlfriend girl

i've realized i would have never been able to leave you.
i'm not a heartbreaker.
i would always think i could fix it,
make us work.

i'm not a casual lover. i'm a kiss-and-tell.
i'm a stalk-you-on-instagram and
write-you-poetry-like-a-fool.
i'm a girlfriend girl.
i don't know how to love any other way,
and i don't really want to.

and if i couldn't break your heart,
i'm glad you broke mine because
fixing us would have broken you too.

perfect apart

i used to worry about
why she got this version of you
and why you changed after we broke up,
but maybe it's just that

i made you the perfect guy
for some other girl,
and you made me
the perfect girl for some future guy.

we weren't perfect together.
we weren't soulmates,
but maybe we helped each other find them.

lover girl

failure

i was so aware, looking back,
that you were unhappy and that
i was unhappy too.
i already knew our time was overdue, but
i couldn't help holding on to this belief
that i could fix us.
i would have been a failure if
we didn't work out.

but here i am,
and i'm not a failure and neither are you,
because even though it's gone,
our love was fire and singing and rain
and it was beautiful.

i will not remember us as a failure.
i will remember us as just
me and you.

capacity for love

i still have that strange
capacity for love.
i can still do it, even now.
and isn't that amazing?
i'm such a romantic, but
i'm a lover girl.
i've never been any other way.

♥

lover girl

my heart still works

my heart still works.
my heart *still* works.
i thought it was unreachable.
i had thought, in some
narcissistic, self-centered way,
that i was stuck like this forever
and that the place that rattled when i breathed
was too small to reach my fingers into
to fix.
i thought that i would be broken
for the rest of my life.

but my heart still works because
i'm standing in the middle of the street
in the night. i'm freezing, but
i can feel the beat of it
down to my toes.

easy

writing about heartbreak is just as easy
as writing about love.

but writing about myself?
that's what hurts the most.

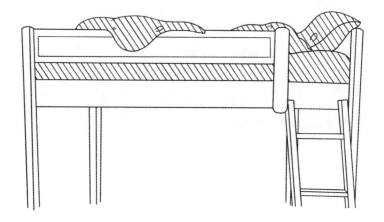

the bed that you built me

i am ripping you from
all the little things.
finally, i am able to wear gray again.
i am able to have my mother rub my back.
i am able to watch *the princess bride*
and can now get into the bed
that you helped me build.
the same one i was in when you called me
and told me
you didn't love me anymore.
here, i am able to sleep.

i am tearing the thoughts of you away from
everything i like.
i like strawberries and the mall.
i like putting my hair in a ponytail. i do.
because after you left,
my mind caught on to all the parts of you it still had:
every place in my room, on my body,
every one that used to be yours.
but now here i am, and they're mine.
my body is finally mine
because in the bed that you built me,
i am able to sleep.

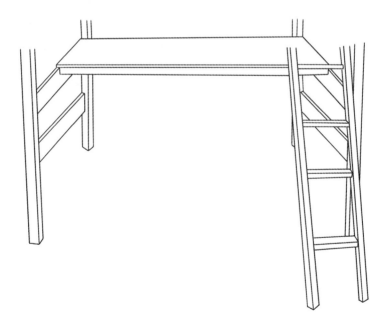

rarity

i have now realized that it's abnormal to be
out with the person you love
every saturday morning and night.
it doesn't happen frequently, that two people
like each other enough to be together so long.

you and i were a rarity.
we were.

and i think i need to recognize that
rarities run out
and one can only be lucky for so long.
i must smile at the past,
and i must move on.

i was lucky to have gotten all the time
i did with you,
but my luck hasn't run out yet.
i know that soon
i will be loved again.

fly

i've realized
i could fly the whole time.
all i needed was to let go of
the comfort of the ground.

all again

you broke me in a way i didn't know
i could break. i've been fixing
broken bones i was unaware existed inside of me
for months. i've lost weight, and
i can't dream the same anymore.
i am not the same as i was.

but if i was ever given the choice,
i would do it all again.

it was still worth it.
every second with you,
every kiss we shared,
every time we danced in the rain,
and every call that went on for hours
was worth the pain, even if that pain
hasn't left me yet.
it was all still worth it.

and i know you know why.
and i know you feel the same.

my first

you were my first,
but you will not be my last.

thought we should talk

i always thought we should talk,
but i think that's for a later time, or
maybe even not at all.

sometime after our hearts have calmed.
it might be in five years, maybe ten.
even though being alive that long from now
seems like a fantasy,
maybe in a later time, or
maybe even not at all,
we could talk about it.

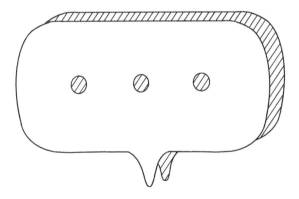

lover girl

i am still lovable

i am going to learn how to love myself again.
if i say it enough times, it'll come true
because love used to be
the only thing on my mind,
and i guess, at the very least,
i need something else to do.

now that i'm letting you go,
there's room in my heart for myself.

i cannot be satisfied with another until i'm
satisfied with my soul
because i won't be happy with a lover boy
if i'm not happy on my own.

so i'm going to learn to love myself again.
i don't exactly know how, but
i know i am still lovable, even if you do not
love me anymore.

even without you,
i am loved.

myself

you changed me.
i'll admit it.
i'm not the same girl i was
before we met.

but i'm not the same girl i was
when you left, either.

that, i did myself.

♥

i will be beautiful

you ripped yourself apart from me,
but i know now that with time
my torn edges will heal.
i will grow back, and i will become
more beautiful than i've ever been.
more beautiful than i was with you.

i will be beautiful,
just you wait.

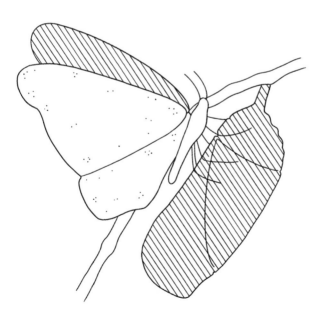

better apart

we're better apart,
and i feel uncomfortable saying it,
but you're happier, and i'm
becoming happier everyday.

the flowers

the flowers can't prick me.
the bees can't sting.
nothing more can hurt me.
no, not a thing.

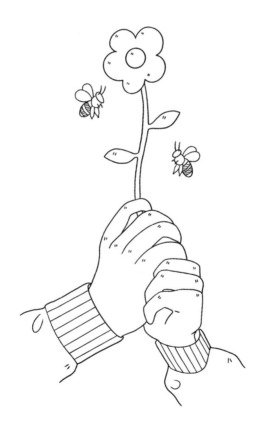

mine

i thought you were mine,
and that's not right.
you could have never been.

because my love for you?
that was always mine.
these words are mine, and
while you were the muse who
dripped them from my lips,
i'm still writing
just like i always used to do.

you were not mine, but
unlike with my heart,
my heartbreak will never be yours.

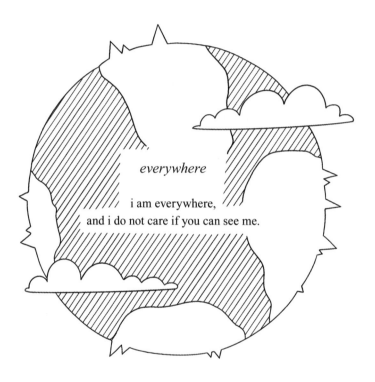

everywhere

i am everywhere,
and i do not care if you can see me.

lover girl

right here

i am thinking of the moment my sister held me
as my tears streamed down my cheeks
onto her nightgown.
it was two in the morning, and i had
woken her up
like a child telling their parents
they had a nightmare.
and as she held me, she whispered
he doesn't deserve you anyways
and i told her
i love him
and she said
i know.

and it was right here
as i'm writing this.
i was right here
but there is no longer salt in my eyes.

my own

my own blood. my own veins.
my own skeleton.
my own muscles and brain.

i do not need your touch
to move my hands anymore.

i can do it all on my own.

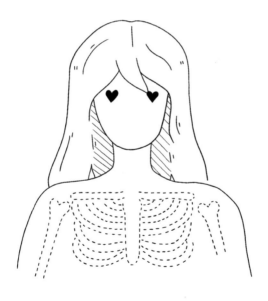

lover girl

just poems

i have hundreds of love poems about you,
but you will never see them.
nobody will ever see them
because last night,

i tore them all apart.
i went through my phone
and deleted every mention of your name.
i deleted every poem i wrote about you,
about your love, about my love for you.
every single one.

i thought, if i held on to them,
i would never forget how love felt.
i would never have to let you go,

and i was a good writer, you know.
my love brought tears to my own eyes.

but i don't need them,
not the way i did before.
they're just some poems.
just poems.
and you know me,
i'll write more.

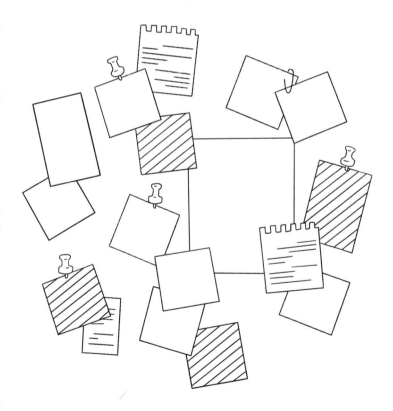

too much

i don't think i loved you too much.
i don't think there is such a thing as
too much love.
but maybe i had fallen so deep in love,
i had forgotten there were things i *liked*.
i had forgotten i could just like something
and that that could have been enough too.

before

i was a poet
before i knew your name,
before i held your hands or kissed your lips.
i was a poet before love,
before heartbreak,
before you.

my voice was my own, even before you.

lover girl

lovers

i have a feeling lover girls and lover boys
exist everywhere.

i find us in
my best friend
and the guy she's in love with
who already has a girlfriend.
i find us in the people at the parties
and the ones who couldn't attend.
in my roommates and my teachers
and the boy at school who looked like you.
in the girl i met in the bathroom
and her ex who found someone new.
in my parents, my grandparents.
in my brother and sister.
i find us in you and her.
and, i guess,
you and me.

we're all just lovers, aren't we?

because i like to think
lover girls and lover boys exist everywhere
if you choose to look for us.

i'm not the only one whose heart was broken this year
and i'm not the only one who put it back together

and neither are you.

lover girl

reckless

i like it,
being reckless with my heart.
nothing could hurt as much as we did,
and i've got nothing else to lose.

how to be happy

i haven't yet discovered
how to be happy
like i searched for desperately when
i was with you
in the touch of your hands
and the feel of your breath on my ear.
how unfair of me was it to ask you
to make me happy
when happiness was not a gift
you could have given me.

lover girl

when

it's no longer a question.

i will be loved again.
it's just a matter of when.

window

i'm caught staring out of my window,
and it surprises me. i'm scared.
i'm scared of heights again.

it's a relief.

lover girl

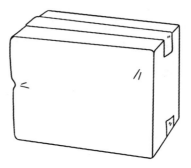

just a thought

today, i got the last of my things from your house.
it's really over now. it is.
i've erased the mention of you from my room
and my phone, and
we don't talk to each other like we used to anymore.
but it's better if it stays like that, isn't it?
it's okay if you're just a thought in my mind
from time to time.

even though we're no longer *you and i,*
we're still alive.
we will survive on different sides of the world.
we will survive apart because
even though it felt as if
your skeleton was inside mine
and i could not feel my lungs without your support,
i don't need your love
to make me breathe anymore.

we're just a thought in my mind
from time to time.

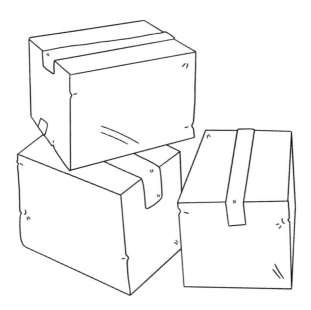

♥

perfectly imperfect

i always used to think i wanted
a perfect love.
that kind of love i see on instagram and
in romance novels,
where he takes me to prom and we post
photos of each other for our monthly anniversaries.
that's what was "perfect" to me.

but we weren't right, and we fought,
and it wasn't perfect.
it was nowhere near perfect,
and yet
the imperfect parts of us are everything i miss
and every reason why i know
we would have never worked.

even though we no longer have
our perfectly imperfect love,
that does not mean
i wanted it to be any other way.

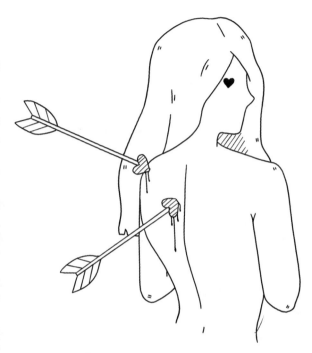

cupid

cupid and i never used to get along,
but i think i get it now.

even after the sting of an arrow,
even after the bandage and the wound,
i'm still here, again and again.
i still let myself get split in two.

"we broke up"

i used to be embarrassed that you left me.
when someone asked me, it would always be
we broke up,
not *he broke up with me.*
maybe then they wouldn't know
if i was crying every night
or they wouldn't think that i was as unwanted
as i felt.

i don't know when it happened,
but i've realized
it's not so bad.
just because you didn't love me back
doesn't make my love embarrassing,
it just means my love wasn't for you.

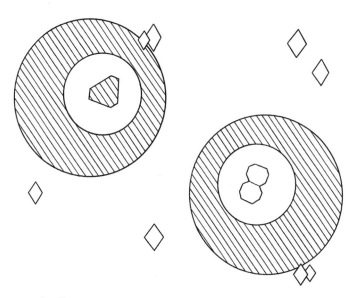

the future

i can try to fool myself with
dice rolls and magic 8 balls,
with acceptance rates and weather reports,
with the stars in the sky and the look in their eyes,
but a poem and a girl can never predict
what comes next.
i'll just have to wait.
i'll just have to wait and see.

but i've got a good feeling about it, i think.
i've got a good feeling about me.

lover girl

love will come to me

love will come to me,
just like you have found each other.
love will come to me,
unlike the falseness i created, selfishly,
between you two.
unlike the love i can feel
less superior to what you already had.
and i will drown in it, when i get my love,
when i finally have what you do.
and when you let me go
(for i will hold on to your less superior love
even after i get my own),
i will go without anger.
i will leave you two to love,
and then
i will leave you two
alone, finally.

open book

i'm a poet. i can't help it.
i talk when i'm happy and
i write when i'm sad.
i share everything with the world, and i like to.
you can read me,
read my heartbreak and foolishness so easily.

but every look of disgust
and every face i receive
doesn't hurt. i never let it hurt
because they're probably just as sensitive as me.
i'm just not afraid to say it.

225

special

heartbreak isn't uncommon.
it's not like i am special because
i loved you and you loved me and then stopped.
it's not like i am the first to ever write
of the feeling, the devastation. the simple
but i thought we were in love.

no. i am not the first and will not be the last.

but if my words can relate, just a little bit,
to someone else's heartbreak,
if my uncommon-common heartbreak
is anything like anyone else's
uncommon-common heartbreak,

then what makes me special isn't
devastation, after all.

a note

i think i like being a lover girl,
even if there's nobody to love right now,
even if my heart gets broken
again and again,
because
love is bigger than just lonely me
and bigger than just heartbreak.
it feels good to love.

even if it hurts,
i don't mind.

acknowledgments

i started writing *Lover Girl* when i turned eighteen
years old. i'd had my first "big break" on tiktok and got
inspired to start writing my first poetry book because
of people supporting me online. the original version
of *Lover Girl* was released only a few months later on
valentine's day. because of the support from my first
followers, i had the motivation to finish it.

i would like to thank other poets i met through the
online poetry space throughout the process. thank you
to whitney hansen, isabella dorta, isabella vedro, and
joey kidney for all of your help in teaching me how
to write a book and pushing me to finish *Lover Girl*
originally. thank you all for your advice and for guiding
me to the new traditional publishing process. i love our
silly "poetry people" group chat, and i love watching
all of your videos as you post online. you guys are my
greatest inspirations and new lifelong friends.

once again, i would like to thank each and every one of my followers for making my dreams possible. from the time i started working on *Lover Girl,* your support has more than doubled, which feels unreal even just writing it down. your support reminds me constantly that poetry is what you make of it, and by simply sharing my work, i can inspire more and more people to write and create more contemporary poetry. i am inspired every day by the work you share with me and the messages i receive in response to my own poetry. thank you, thank you, thank you.

finally, i want to specifically thank each person who bought the original version of *Lover Girl* and is reading this version now. thank you for following me through my journey of writing this book, from start to finish, and i hope you enjoyed this version even more than the original. you mean the world to me, really.

♥

about the author

raegan fordemwalt is a nineteen-year-old poet from the vibrant city of boise, idaho, and is currently a college student studying in california. she started writing poetry during her early teenage years and fell in love with the craft. she started posting her poetry online a few years later and found massive success on platforms like instagram and tiktok. throughout her year and a half of posting online, she gained over four million collective followers and over a hundred million likes and hearts across both platforms. raegan has inspired thousands of young writers to share their work online.

Lover Girl is her first published collection. she originally self-published the work as a senior in high school, and it reached #1 in multiple categories on amazon during its first week of publication. *Lover Girl* draws inspiration from her own experiences as a young woman learning to navigate love and heartbreak.

raegan believes that poetry can be made from anything, whether that be a broken heart or just a weird pebble on the street. you can find more of her work online via her tiktok and instagram, @raeganspoetry.

❤